PICTURING SCOTLAND

DISTINGUISHED DISTILLERIES

NESS PUBLISHING

2 Royal Lochnagar Distillery, Royal Deeside.

DISTINGUISHED DISTILLERIES

Welcome to the world of whisky!

Whisky, especially Malt Whisky, stirs many emotions and memories. It is not just the whisky, but who you are enjoying it with, and perhaps the place, which engenders that special camaraderie. Whisky is a very social drink that encourages you to appreciate its many complexities and characteristics. We enjoy whisky to celebrate births, marriages and often at funerals where the departed has prescribed his or her favourite dram to be enjoyed after the ceremony. I was first introduced to whisky at a sporting occasion; my memory does not allow me to recollect whether I was celebrating or commiserating ... but that's part of the enjoyment! Whisky has a canny character that makes it appropriate at any event.

Scotland's distilleries are an integral part of the country's history and an engine of its economy. This book takes you on an illustrated tour of 40 of the most notable distilleries, from Islay in the south-west to Orkney in the far north, with many mainland establishments in between. It is created both for the armchair traveller and for those touring Scotland with the particular aim of visiting the many distilleries that welcome visitors. Each one will tell you its stories and share its secrets. Each presentation is unique but each one shares its passion for the 'water of life'.

The Famous Grouse at Glenturret Distillery. **5**

Enjoying Whisky

The most important way is your way! But I would encourage you to experiment with a little water; you decide whether it is a splash or a drop. A little water is an important means of helping you to appreciate fully the whisky you are drinking. It opens the whisky up and allows your taste buds to do their job. It will take a little practice, but you will learn to distinguish the many flavours each whisky can deliver.

There are five different whisky producing regions in Scotland: Highland, Lowland, Speyside, Islay and Campbeltown. Although there are variations within each region, for the most part there is an underlying 'signature' taste and style to the whiskies produced in each one. Speyside is located within the Highland region and therefore whiskies produced there can be labelled as either Highland or Speyside.

The boundary that defines where the Lowlands end and the Highlands begin is known as the 'Highland Line'. It runs between the Clyde and Tay rivers (approximately from Perth to Greenock). Broadly speaking, everywhere to the north of this line is classed as Highland, although the exact

In the new Still House at The Glenlivet Distillery.

course of the line has varied down the years. The origins of the Highland Line go back to the 17th century when it was intended to help reduce tax evasion in the remoter parts of Scotland, where most whisky distilling was carried out illicitly, and on which, therefore, no tax was paid. This meant that distilleries in the Lowlands bore the brunt of the tax burden. In an attempt to 'level the playing field', an Act of Parliament in 1784 imposed different rates of tax on each side of the line, with a lower tariff for the Lowland distillers. This then influenced where some distilleries were built and is thus part of the story of some of the distilleries we shall visit.

Scotland exports whisky to all corners of the world so you can enjoy a little bit of Scotland anywhere from Adelaide to Zurich. So wherever you are, *slàinte mhath!*

Finally, a gentle reminder that drinking and driving should never be encouraged while touring distilleries, so please have a dedicated driver while touring and tasting. Or better still, employ the services of a driver-guide so you can all immerse yourselves in the search for your favourite malt.

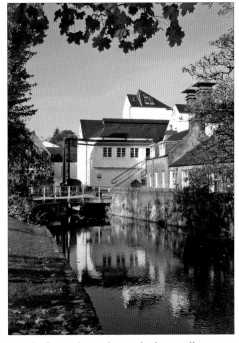

The River Isla flows through Strathisla Distillery.

Ardbeg (Glenmorangie Co Ltd)

Region: Islay

Tel No: 01496 302244

Address: Port Ellen, Isle of Islay, PA42 7EA

Web Address: www.ardbeg.com

Founded in 1815 by John MacDougall, Ardbeg has had a chequered history. Since reaching a production peak of 1.1million litres of whisky in1887, it has changed hands a few times and been closed twice. However, with current owners The House of Glenmorangie and Moet Hennessey Louis Vuitton, by 2005 it had emulated the production quantities of 1887. The past few years have firmly established Ardbeg as an award-winning whisky with various expressions being awarded Whisky of the Year by the prestigious whisky writer Jim Murray. This includes the 10 Year Old Ardbeg Single Malt, the heart of the Ardbeg family.

Colour, Nose and Tasting Notes:
Ardbeg 10 Year Old

The colour is light gold, on the nose there is immediate intense smoke, mixed with soft peat, and a sea breeze. On the palate it is clean, fresh, with medicinal notes and a light maltiness. The smoke is pleasant and there is a long dry finish.

Ardbeg Distillery.   9

Lagavulin (Diageo)

Region: Islay

Tel No: 01496 302749

Address: Port Ellen, Isle of Islay, PA42 7DZ

Web Address: www.malts.com

In 1816 John Johnston, a local farmer and distiller, founded Lagavulin Distillery. With the abundance of peat bogs on the west of the island, Lagavulin became famous for its heavily peated barley aromas. With a longer than average distillation process and with the most popular bottling of Lagavulin being the 16 Year Old, it is said that this enhances the aromas and flavours. Lagavulin is a long established classic from Islay which has the peat, the sea and the smoke all beautifully balanced in a great whisky.

Colour, Nose and Tasting Notes:
Lagavulin 16 Year Old

A deep amber gold colour and the nose is rich with smoke aromas infused with seaweed and hints of medicinal iodine. The peaty taste leads to the sea saltiness of smoked fish with sweetness from dried fruit. A complex whisky to savour at leisure.

Lagavulin Distillery.

Laphroaig (Beam Global Spirits & Wine)

Region: Islay

Tel No: 01496 302418

Address: Port Ellen, Isle of Islay, PA42 7DU

Web Address: www.laphroaig.com

This is the smokiest and most phenolic of all the Islay whiskies. Laphroaig translates to mean beautiful hollow by the broad bay. Founded in 1810 by the brothers Alexander and Donald Johnston, it officially started producing in 1815, reportedly after the excise men became suspicious! Because of its pungent aroma and smoky flavour, Laphroaig is an acquired taste loved by many. This is a whisky with eminent followers including Prince Charles, Duke of Rothesay, who gave his Royal Warrant to Laphroaig in 1994.

Colour, Nose and Tasting Notes:
Laphroaig 10 Year Old

The colour is a pale golden yellow with aromas of seaweed, medicinal notes and peat smoke. It is very powerful on the nose. The palate comes alive with salty, creosote and peat flavours, with a long dry finish – a true classic!

Laphroaig Distillery. 13

Bowmore (Morrison Bowmore Distillers Ltd)

Region: Islay

Tel No: 01496 810671

Address: School Street, Bowmore, Isle of Islay, PA43 7JS

Web Address: bowmore.com

This is the oldest distillery on Islay, founded in 1779. It is picturesquely located close to Bowmore harbour on Loch Indaal. Bowmore can be considered a rarity in that it still produces and malts up to 40% of its own barley. Most distillers buy in their malted barley from specialist maltsters. Bowmore Distillery also matures most of its whisky in Sherry casks, which is unusual amongst the distillers on Islay, the majority of which use a mix of Sherry and American Bourbon casks.

Colour, Nose and Tasting Notes:
Bowmore 12 Year Old

A warm amber colour, reflecting the Sherry casks in which it has been matured. There is smoke and peat on the nose but also hints of lemon and sweetness of heather honey. On the palate it has a smoky and sweet peaty taste with hints of chocolate and spice, with a long and lingering finish.

14   Bowmore Distillery.

Kilchoman (Kilchoman Distillery Co Ltd)

Region: Islay   **Address:** Rockside Farm, Bruichladdich, Isle of Islay, PA49 7UT
Tel No: 01496 850011   **Web Address:** www.kilchomandistillery.com

Established in 2005, this is the first distillery to be constructed on Islay since 1908. It is the smallest distillery on Islay producing just 100,000 litres per year. However, it has already won awards for its whisky, and is unique in that all the barley is grown on the farm adjacent to the distillery, where it is malted, distilled, matured and even bottled!

A young whisky, the Inaugural Bottling is just 3 years old, although Kilchoman is regularly releasing new bottlings some vatted with 4-year-old whisky, a practice that will probably continue as the whisky matures. A pioneering distillery that will continue to grow and develop.

Colour, Nose and Tasting Notes:
Kilchoman Spring 2011 Release

The colour is very pale straw and the nose is of subtle peat mixed with ripe berries and light oak. On the palate the smoke is very subtle, with the berries dominating along with toffee notes and vanilla.

Kilchoman Vintage 2006 Release.   **15**

Caol Ila (Diageo)

Region: Islay

Tel No: 01496 302760

Address: Port Askaig, Isle of Islay, PA46 7RL

Web Address: www.malts.com

Located close to Port Askaig, Caol Ila (pronounced Cull Eela) is the largest distillery on Islay. For almost 100 years the whisky was taken by ship directly from the distillery to the mainland through the sound of Islay – Caol Ila in Gaelic. Nowadays it is taken by lorry to the ferry and although there is warehousing at the distillery, much of the whisky is matured on the mainland. Caol Ila is a heavily peated, powerful whisky, typical of most Islay whiskies.

Colour, Nose and Tasting Notes:
Caol Ila 12 Year Old

Pale straw in colour, this whisky is full of peat smoke on the nose with hints of sea air, and a little almond. The palate is oily, slightly medicinal with smoke and some dried fruits.

Caol Ila Distillery. **17**

Bunnahabhain (Burn Stewart Distillers Ltd)

Region: Islay   **Address: Port Askaig, Isle of Islay, PA46 7RP**

Tel No: 01496 840646   **Web Address:** www.bunnahabhain.com & www.blackbottle.com

Built between 1881 and 1893 by the Greenlees brothers and now owned by Burn Stewart Distillers Ltd, Bunnahabhain Distillery is located at the northern end of Islay, reached by a single-track road which can make driving interesting if you meet a lorry coming towards you!

A considerable amount of the production goes into the famous blended Black Bottle Whisky. Unlike many of the Islay distilleries, Bunnahabhain does not have a hugely peaty aroma. This is because its water is piped directly from its limestone source and they do not use heavily peated barley. It is a soft, fruity malt, with a hint of the sea.

Colour, Nose and Tasting Notes:
Bunnahabhain 12 Year Old

Deep gold in colour, and a nose full of freshness with only a subtle reference to smoke, on the palate there are nutty and light fruit flavours with some malt and gentle smoke. The finish is quite short but pleasant.

Bunnahabhain Distillery. **19**

Jura (Whyte and Mackay Ltd)

Region: Highlands (Jura)
Tel No: 01496 820601

Address: Craighouse, Isle of Jura, Argyll, PA60 7XT
Web Address: www.isleofjura.com

Established in 1810 by Archibald Campbell and located in the settlement of Craighouse (the main village on the island), it is only accessible via the neighbouring island of Islay. Jura whisky is known as the 'Highland from the Island'. It is very different from the whiskies produced on Islay as much less peat, if any, is used in most of the production. Owned by Whyte and Mackay, it went through a transformation when it was decided to re-rack the whisky as many of the casks in the warehouses were not up to standard. This change, along with Master Blender Richard Paterson's expert nose, led to the creation in recent years of several new expressions, all of which have been well received.

Colour, Nose and Tasting Notes:
Jura 10 year old

Clear bright gold in colour, the nose is slightly oily, with subtle salt and pine. The palate is sweet with honey overtones, malt and sea salt. The finish is lingering and pleasant.

Isle of Jura Distillery. **21**

Glenkinchie (Diageo)

Region: Lowland

Tel No: 01875 342004

Address: Pencaitland, Tranent, East Lothian, EH34 5ET

Web Address: www.discovering-distilleries.com

Glenkinchie, also known as Edinburgh's distillery, is one of only five Lowland distilleries left in production. Although Lowland whisky is not as well known as some of the Highland and Speyside distilleries, the region was once at the heart of the whisky industry: in 1837 there were 115 distilleries in the Lowlands. Lowland whisky had the advantage of better roads and links to the north and south and also excellent agricultural land to ensure a plentiful supply of barley.

Colour, Nose and Tasting Notes:
Glenkinchie 12 Year Old

Mid gold in colour, Glenkinchie has light, grassy aromas that are fresh with hints of floral and smoke. It is dry on the palate, with plenty of malt and a long and dry finish.

One of the superb models at Glenkinchie Distillery in the exhibition which shows how whisky is made. **23**

Glengoyne (Ian MacLeod Distillers Ltd)

Region: Southern Highlands **Address: Dumgoyne, Nr Killearn, Glasgow, G63 9LB**

Tel No: 01360 550254 Web Address: www.glengoyne.com

Glengoyne Distillery is a very pretty distillery in the southern highlands north of Glasgow. It takes its name from Glen Guin, meaning Glen of the Wild Geese. It has been in continuous production since 1833 and has always remained owned by Scottish Companies. Today it is owned by Ian Macleod Distillers Limited and carries a Royal Warrant. Intriguingly, the Highland Line is drawn such that Glengoyne Distillery is split in two, with the result that the whisky is produced in the Highlands but matured in the Lowlands!

Colour, Nose and Tasting Notes:
The Glengoyne 12 Year Old

A gold appearance reminiscent of a sweet pudding wine. With oak, almonds, tropical fruits and boiled sweets on the nose you can't wait to taste it. It does not disappoint; a clean, smooth, well-rounded single malt with Sherry notes, hints of chocolate and a long creamy, fruity finish.

Glengoyne Distillery. **25**

Tullibardine (Picard Family)

Region: Highland **Address:** The Tullibardine Distillery, Blackford, Perthshire, PH4 1QG
Tel No: 01764 682252 **Web Address:** www.tullibardine.com

Set against the stunning backdrop of the Ochil Hills, Tullibardine has only been a distillery since the 1940s, originally being a brewery that dated back to 1488. It famously sold beer to King James IV following his coronation at Scone Palace. Welshman William Evans converted it into a distillery following his purchase of the business in 1947. He had also designed the Isle of Jura Distillery. A committed engineer, he designed the distillery to maximise efficiency and used nature where possible: to this day, water is fed over the cooling condensers by gravity. Mothballed for a period of time, it was bought by a consortium of businessmen in 2003 and is now fully operational. After eight years as custodians they recently sold to the Picard family from France, thus beginning a new chapter in Tullibardine's history.

Colour, Nose and Tasting Notes:
Tullibardine Aged Oak Edition

A light pale gold colour, with youthful barley on the nose, citrus and pear drop flavours, with a hint of toasted vanilla.

A selection of vintage whiskies from Tullibardine Distillery. **27**

Glenturret - The Famous Grouse Experience (The Edrington Group)

Region: Eastern Highlands   **Address:** The Hosh, Crieff, Perthshire, PH7 4HA

Tel No: 01764 656565   **Web Address:** www.thefamousgrouse.com

Arguably the oldest distillery in Scotland, Glenturret Distillery can be dated back to 1775 when whisky smugglers created a small, illicit still. Glenturret, formerly known as Hosh Distillery, is the established home of the Famous Grouse blended whisky and welcomes tens of thousands of visitors every year. Most of the whisky produced is used for blending and Famous Grouse is the top-selling blended whisky in Scotland. Originally named 'Grouse' whisky in 1896 by Perthshire merchant Matthew Gloag, who added the word 'Famous' in 1905 following the enormous popularity of the blend he had created. There are a few limited bottlings of single malt, notably the 10 Year Old. Glenturret is also famous for its cat Towser, who made it in to the Guinness Book of Records for killing 28,899 mice. She lived for 24 years and only the kills found near the stills were counted. Her other victims included pheasants and rabbits!

Colour, Nose and Tasting Notes:
The Glenturret 10 Year Old

Pale amber in colour, on the nose it is fresh, fruity and with aromas of barley. The palate is fruity with a hint of nuts with some honey sweetness. Not a long finish, but a very pleasant classic malt.

Glenturret Distillery, home of the Famous Grouse. **29**

Oban (Diageo)

Region: Western Highlands

Tel No: 01631 572004

Address: Stafford Street, Oban, Argyll, PA34 5NH

Web Address: www.discovering-distilleries.com

Located in the centre of the west highland town of the same name, Oban Distillery is said to have been in existence before the town and that the town grew around it. It certainly sits in the heart of Oban and therefore there is no opportunity to expand, with buildings on three sides and a steep rock face on the other. Close to the harbour and looking over towards the Isle of Mull, Oban Distillery has just two stills which limit production, but this small distillery produces quality whisky that is used only for single malts, the 14 Year Old being one of the most popular.

Colour, Nose and Tasting Notes:
Oban 14 Year Old

Rich gold in colour, with coastal sea-salt aromas, light peat and some honey notes. The taste is well rounded with some toffee, sherried oak, autumn fruits, some more peat smoke and the finish is long and smooth.

Oban Distillery. **31**

Tobermory (Burn Stewart Distillers Ltd)

Region: Highland (Mull)
Tel No: 01688 302647

Address: Tobermory, Isle of Mull, PA75 6NR
Web Address: www.tobermorymalt.com

Started in 1798 by John Sinclair, Tobermory Distillery was owned for a short time by the same company that owned Oban Distillery. Over the last 200 years it has spent many years closed, either through bankruptcy or refurbishment. Located close to the harbour in the picturesque town of Tobermory, it is now producing two very different whiskies. Tobermory is distilled from unpeated barley, very unusual for an island whisky, and matured for a minimum of 10 years. Ledaig, distilled from peated barley, is cut from the spirit still at a lower alcohol content to retain the powerful peaty flavours.

Colour, Nose and Tasting Notes:
Tobermory 10 Year Old

Pale amber in colour with a fresh lightly smoky nose, grassy with oak and vanilla notes. The taste is smooth, fruity and very well rounded.

Tobermory Distillery. **33**

Located on the edge of the picturesque town of Aberfeldy and close to the River Tay, this distillery was founded by John and Tommy Dewar in 1896. They were following in their father's footsteps, who had set up his own spirits business and knew that money could be made from whisky, having been blending and selling his own successfully for many years. In order to continue to produce and ensure the quality of their best-selling Dewar's White Label, they built Aberfeldy Distillery which to this day provides the base malt for this famous blend.

Colour, Nose and Tasting Notes:
Aberfeldy 12 Year Old

The colour is amber and the nose is rich and rounded with aromas of cereal, heather honey, slightly smoky, with hints of toffee. The palate is warmed with flavours of honey, spices and citrus. The finish is long and drying.

Aberfeldy Distillery, home of Dewar's World of Whisky. The distillery used to operate its own steam **35** shunting locomotive back when Aberfeldy was on the rail network. It can be seen on the left.

Blair Athol (Diageo)

Region: Eastern Highlands
Tel No: 01796 482003

Address: Pitlochry, Perthshire, PH16 5LY
Web Address: www.discovering-distilleries.com

The first known distillery on this site was in 1798 when John Stewart and Robert Robertson built a distillery here called Aldour, named after the Allt Dour burn meaning 'burn of the otter'. When the First World War broke out, the men working at the distillery were sent off to war with a free bottle and the women continued to make the whisky. However, when prohibition was imposed in the USA, trade disappeared and the distillery closed. In 1933 it was bought by Arthur Bell and Son, although it remained closed during the Second World War. It re-opened in 1945 and has been in production ever since. It has always been used as part of the Bell's blend since the 1850s when Arthur Bell would travel around distilleries experimenting with blending.

Colour, Nose and Tasting Notes:
Blair Athol 12 Year Old

The colour is a rich amber and the nose is mellow with Sherry, spice and citrus fruit. The palate is full bodied, with dried fruits, citrus and a sweetness of caramel. The finish is warming and long.

Blair Athol Distillery, flying the flag for Bell's. **37**

Ben Nevis (Ben Nevis Distillery (Fort William) Ltd)

Region: Western Highlands
Tel No: 01397 700200
Address: Lochy Bridge, Fort William, PH33 6TJ
Web Address: www.bennevisdistillery.com

Lying at the foot of Britain's highest mountain, Ben Nevis, on the outskirts of Fort William, it was established in 1825 by John Macdonald. The distillery has had a chequered history, having been closed twice, but has gone from strength to strength since being acquired in 1989 by Nikka Distilling Company from Japan. As well as producing a single malt, its whisky also forms an integral part in the blended Dew of Ben Nevis.

Colour, Nose and Tasting Notes:
Ben Nevis 10 Year Old

Pale amber in colour, on the nose there are subtle hints of orange and smoky peatiness. The palate is full with the complexities of toffee, hints of chocolate, oak and as it lingers, fruity notes appear. The finish is long, pleasant and malty.

Dalwhinnie (Diageo)

Region: Northern Highlands

Tel No: 01540 672219

Address: Dalwhinnie, Inverness-shire, PH19 1AB

Web Address: www.malts.com

Colour, Nose and Tasting Notes:
Dalwhinnie 15 Year Old

Has a crisp dry nose with subtle hints of peat and heather. It is an elegant, mellow, gentle malt with soft honey sweetness, citrus notes and a long smooth finish.

The name Dalwhinnie comes for the Gaelic for a 'meeting place' for cattle and sheep drovers. The mountains that surround Dalwhinnie Distillery are both dramatic and beautiful: this is where the Cairngorms meet the Monadhliath Mountains and where you will find Scotland's second-highest distillery, Dalwhinnie. Founded in 1897 and originally called Strathspey, one can only hazard a guess as to why such a wild and windswept location was chosen for a whisky distillery. However, as well as having an ample supply of spring water, its remoteness was lessened by the arrival of the Highland Railway line, which offered a safe and regular distribution link to get the whisky to market.

40 Dalwhinnie Distillery at night.

Royal Lochnagar (Diageo)

Region: Eastern Highlands

Tel No: 01339 742700

Address: Crathie, Ballatar, Aberdeenshire, AB35 5TB

Web Address: www.discovering-distilleries.com

Originally named Lochnagar, it was founded in 1823 by James Robertson at a time when the Lochnagar mountains were still home to many whisky smugglers. The distillery was burnt down twice between 1826 and 1841. However, it benefited from Queen Victoria and Prince Albert's purchase of the adjacent Balmoral Castle. Following a visit to the distillery by the Royal couple, Lochnagar became an official supplier to the Crown and therefore could add the 'Royal' prefix to its name.

Colour, Nose and Tasting Notes:
Royal Lochnagar 12 Year Old

Rich old gold colour, a whisper of toffee and woody notes on the nose. The palate has flavours of malty sweetness, Sherry and a hint of smoke. Good balance with a medium finish.

Royal Lochnagar Distillery. **43**

Glen Garioch (Morrison Bowmore Distillers Ltd)

Region: Eastern Highlands **Address:** Distillery Road, Old Meldrum, Aberdeenshire, AB51 0ES
Tel No: 01651 873450 **Web Address:** www.glengarioch.com

John and Alexander Manson founded Glen Garioch distillery in 1797. Pronounced Glen Geery, the distillery was located next to a brewery. The Manson brothers, like many new distillers, came from a farming family. John Manson and his wife Elizabeth's second son, Patrick, found recognition after graduating in medicine from Aberdeen University when he discovered a direct link between mosquitoes and malaria. Over the past two hundred years, Glen Garioch has been transferred to various owners and been closed due to a shortage of water. A new spring was subsequently found. In the 1970s, in response to escalating fuel costs, the owners developed a system of using waste heat from the distillery to power an acre of greenhouses and an acre of polytunnels to produce vegetables. Over the last few years the brand has been completely revamped and the 12 Year Old is matured in both Bourbon and Sherry casks.

Colour, Nose and Tasting Notes:
Glen Garioch 12 Year Old

The colour is a deep gold, with suggestions of tropical fruit sweetness on the nose, with Sherry and some vanilla. When tasted, sweetness remains alongside vanilla, oak and some spice. The finish is soft and long with a little spice.

44 See p.80 for picture of Glen Garioch Distillery.

Tomatin (Tomatin Distillery Co Ltd)

Region: Highland
Tel No: 01463 248144

Address: Tomatin, Inverness-shire, IV13 7YT
Web Address: www.tomatin.com

Started by a group of Inverness businessmen during the whisky boom of late 1800s, Tomatin Distillery is on the eastern edge of the Monadhliath Mountains. It is located on an old drovers' trail and can date selling illegal whisky back to the 15th century when drovers would fill a flask from a still at the Old Laird's House. Tomatin was once the largest distillery in Scotland, having grown rapidly in the 1960s and 70s when production reached 12 million litres of alcohol. It is also unusual in that it employs its own coopers to repair casks, and many of the families who work at the distillery also live in houses provided for them. Tomatin is a real community whisky.

Colour, Nose and Tasting Notes:
Tomatin 12 Year Old
A colour of warm gold, a whisky that has orchard fruits and a little smokiness on the nose, smooth and silky on the palate with a hint of nuttiness.

One of the stills at Tomatin Distillery.

Talisker (Diageo)

Region: Highlands (Skye)

Tel No: 01478 614308

Address: Carbost, Isle of Skye, IV47 8SR

Web Address: www.discovering-distilleries.com

Talisker is the only distillery on the Isle of Skye. It is protected from the stormy Atlantic Ocean by its sheltered location at Carbost near the head of Loch Harport. Built in 1830 by brothers Hugh and Kenneth MacAskill, it did not stay in their hands for very long before being taken over. Making it a viable business proved difficult, probably due to its location; matters were made worse when one owner's agent was imprisoned for selling casks that did not exist! Talisker was triple-distilled (spirit is normally distilled twice) until the late 1920s. In 1960 the Still House burnt down leaving it with no production for two years, but fortunately the warehouses remained untouched. Since Talisker 10 Year Old became part of Diageo's Classic Malt collection it has become very popular and the visitor centre welcomes over 50,000 visitors annually.

Colour, Nose and Tasting Notes:
Talisker 10 Year Old

Bright gold in appearance and packed with peaty smokiness on the nose and more than a hint of the sea. The palate is full of billowing smoke and peaty barley, there is some dried fruit lingering in the back-ground and a definite long warming finish.

Talisker Distillery.

The Glenlivet (Chivas Brothers)

Region: Speyside • Address: Glenlivet, Ballindalloch, Banffshire, AB37 9DB

Tel No: 01340 821720   Web Address: www.theglenlivet.com & www.maltwhiskydistilleries.com

A farmer by the name of George Smith (see picture on p.4) founded Glenlivet in 1824 in one of Speyside's remotest glens. It has a fascinating story that tells of heroic acts. George Smith carried pistols to protect himself from the smugglers who resented his pioneering shift from illicit to licensed distiller. His whisky was considered the very best, even being asked for by name by King George IV on his state visit to Edinburgh in 1822. Other distilleries tried to copy and added the name 'Glenlivet' to their own whisky in an effort to signify that theirs too was whisky of very high quality. After much legal wrangling over many years, owner John Gordon Smith won the case and there is now only one whisky worthy of the name The Glenlivet.

Colour, Nose and Tasting Notes:
The Glenlivet 12 Year Old

The colour is a bright gold, with tropical fruits and full bloom heather on the nose. Malty on the palate with hints of vanilla and oak, a medium finish with hints of spice and almonds.

The Glenlivet Distillery. **49**

Cragganmore (Diageo)

Region: Speyside
Tel No: 01479 874635

Address: Ballindalloch, Banffshire, AB37 9AB
Web Address: www.discovering-distilleries.com

Cragganmore distillery nestles in a pretty glen in the heart of Speyside close to Ballindalloch Castle. Founded in 1869 by the very experienced John Smith, who had previously run Glenfarclas and Ballindalloch distilleries. In the 1920s it was partly owned by Ballindalloch Estate. Cragganmore has set itself apart from others by having very unusual flat-topped stills which, along with the worm tubs that cool the vapours, all help to create a complex whisky that is very aromatic. Most of its production is sent for blending and it is used in the White Horse blend amongst others.

Colour, Nose and Tasting Notes:

Cragganmore 12 Year Old

Straw gold in appearance with floral and herb aromas on the nose, it is a dry whisky with woody, maltiness notes and some orange fruit. There is a little smoke and peat on the finish.

50 Whisky maturing at Cragganmore Distillery.

Glenfarclas (J & B Grant)

Region: Speyside
Tel No: 01807 500257

Address: Ballindalloch, Banffshire, AB37 9BD
Web Address: www.glenfarclas.co.uk

Founded in 1836 by Robert Hay, bought in 1865 by the Grant Family and now being run by the sixth generation of the family, Glenfarclas has a renowned reputation for excellence of quality. While most production is concentrated on producing single malt, it is much sought after by blenders for its consistent quality. In 1968 Glenfarclas was also the first to introduce a cask-strength whisky. Latterly named Glenfarclas 105, it was ahead of its time as it was thought that there would not be a market for a cask-strength single malt. Glenfarclas also led the way in being one of the first to create a visitor centre.

Colour, Nose and Tasting Notes:
Glenfarclas 105 Cask Strength

A deep golden colour and bottled at 60% ABV, this whisky needs a little water to take away the fiery alcohol, leaving you with a dram that has aromas that are oakey, with ripe orchard fruits. On the palate it is rich with sherried fruits and very smooth for the strength. A lingering finish with a hint of smoke.

A retired still makes a striking feature **51** at Glenfarclas Distillery.

Cardhu (Diageo)

Region: Speyside
Tel No: 01479 874635

Address: Knockando, Moray, AB38 7RY
Web Address: www.discovering-distilleries.com

Cardhu was started in 1824 by John Cummings, a former whisky smuggler whose original distillery was sited higher up on the Mannoch Hill. The distillery was mainly run by his wife, Helen, who would sell the whisky from the farm house. It moved to the existing site in 1885 and was operated as a farm distillery using its own barley. By this time it was being managed by Helen's daughter-in-law, Elizabeth – women's involvement in whisky production was very unusual at this time. When the new distillery was built, the old stills were sold to William Grant who used them to found Glenfiddich Distillery. Over the years, as production increased, more of Cardhu's high quality single malt was purchased by Johnnie

Walker & Sons to be used in their blends. In 1893 Elizabeth sold the distillery to Johnnie Walker & Sons and it is now the established home of Johnnie Walker blended whisky, although Cardhu continues to produce a single malt.

Colour, Nose and Tasting Notes:

Cardhu 12 Year Old

Pale straw in colour with light, floral notes, hints of orchard pears, a malty nutty palate with sweetness of toffee and a small amount of peat. A medium length of finish that is crisp.

Cardhu Distillery, set amongst the barley fields that historically have provided **53** this raw material for its whisky.

Aberlour (Chivas Brothers)

Region: Speyside

Tel No: 01340 881249

Address: High Street, Aberlour, Banffshire, AB38 9PJ

Web Address: www.aberlour.com

Aberlour Distillery sits in the heart of Speyside, arguably Scotland's finest whisky-making area. Two thirds of all active distilleries are located around Speyside. Founded in 1826 by James Gordon and Peter Weir, it was acquired by grain merchant James Fleming following a fire, after which it was rebuilt in its current location. James Fleming was a man who worked hard at putting something back into the community that had served him so well. He financed the construction of Aberlour Town Hall, the Cottage Hospital and the Penny Bridge. Aberlour also 'double casks' most of its whisky: some is matured in Sherry butts and some in Bourbon casks before being married together to produce an excellent Speyside Single Malt.

Colour, Nose and Tasting Notes:
Aberlour 10 Year Old

Rich gold in colour, with aromas of Sherry and sweet orchard apples. On the palate it is rich with Christmas cake spices, toffee and Sherry sweetness leading to a lingering warm finish with a subtle spice.

The Gatehouse at Aberlour Distillery. **55**

The Macallan (The Edrington Group)

Region: Speyside

Tel No: 01340 872280

Address: Craigellachie, Aberlour, AB38 9RX

Web Address: www.themacallan.com

The Macallan Distillery sits high above the River Spey with majestic views across to Ben Rinnes. Like some other distilleries on Speyside it was founded by a farmer, Alexander Reid, who leased the land from the Earl of Seafield. It is thought that the Macallan name comes from two Gaelic words, 'Magh' meaning fertile piece of ground and 'Ellan' meaning 'of St Fillan', an Irish-born monk who evangelized Scotland in the eighth century. Macallan has always produced whisky of exceptional quality, ensuring all their casks are imported from Jerez in Spain after first being used for Olorosso Sherry, making it one of the most popular single malts globally.

Colour, Nose and Tasting Notes:

The Macallan 12 Year Old Sherry Oak

Matured for a minimum of 12 years in Sherry Oak Casks, this rich gold whisky has plenty of rich Christmas Cake aromas and this follows through to the taste where it is rich and warming with plenty of fruit and spice, with a long lingering finish.

The Macallan Distillery sits on the hillside above the River Spey near Craigellachie. **57**
Ben Rinnes (840m/2755ft) is in the distance.

Glenfiddich (William Grant & Sons Ltd)

Region: Speyside

Address: Dufftown, Banffshire, AB55 4DH

Tel No: 01340 820373

Web Address: www.glenfiddich.com

Glenfiddich is in Dufftown, the whisky capital of Speyside. Founded in 1886 by William Grant who had worked previously for Mortlach Distillery, learning the trade as a young boy and working his way up to become distillery manager. The first spirit ran from the stills at Glenfiddich Distillery on Christmas Day 1887 – it had taken William Grant and his family little over a year to construct a distillery. It is now the whisky with the most awards and once tasted, it's easy to understand why. Glenfiddich means 'Valley of the Deer', hence the impressive stag's head on the famous logo.

Colour, Nose and Tasting Notes:
Glenfiddich 15 Year Old

The 15 Year Old is matured in three different types of oak cask: Sherry, Bourbon and new oak, before being 'married' together. The result is a delicious whisky with heather honey, vanilla and toffee flavours and a hint of spice, very festive for Christmas!

Glenfiddich Distillery. **59**

Glen Grant (Glen Grant Distillery Co)

Region: Speyside

Tel No: 01340 832118

Address: Rothes, Moray, AB38 7BS

Web Address: www.glengrant.com

Glen Grant distillery is located in the Speyside town of Rothes, where there are several distilleries. Founded in 1840 by brothers James and John Grant, who had previously managed Dandaleith Distillery. By 1897 the family had expanded the distillery and created a new one across the road that was named Glen Grant No.2, but sadly it was mothballed just five years later. It wasn't until 1965 that production restarted at Glen Grant No.2 and it was renamed Caperdonich. Since 1965 there have been several owners, including Chivas and Diageo. It is now owned by Campari and is a very popular single malt in Italy. Their most popular single malt is the 10 Year Old. In recent years they have focused on the American market.

Colour, Nose and Tasting Notes:
Glen Grant 10 Year Old

Barley gold in colour with vanilla and orchard apples on the nose. The taste is fruity with a gentle nuttiness and a medium length of finish.

Glen Grant Distillery is famous for its fine gardens as well as its excellent whisky. **61**
Left: the burn (stream) that provides the distillery's water source. Right: the distillery pond.

Strathisla (Chivas Brothers)

Region: Speyside

Address: Seafield Avenue, Keith, Banffshire, AB55 5BS

Tel No: 01542 783044

Web Address: www.chivas.com & www.maltwhiskydistilleries.com

Arguably the prettiest distillery on Speyside, Strathisla is situated in the town of Keith. It is the spiritual home of Chivas Regal Blended Whisky and, as such, there is more emphasis on this than on the single malt of Strathisla. Founded in 1786, it has had a turbulent history that includes a major fire in 1876, followed some years later by an explosion and one owner being jailed for black market dealings which led to bankruptcy in 1949. Following the bankruptcy, the company that also owned Chivas Brothers acquired the distillery at auction in 1950 and have invested substantially since then. Alongside increasing the number of stills to boost output, the historic buildings have been restored and maintained to a high standard.

Colour, Nose and Tasting Notes:
The Strathisla 12 Year Old

Gold in colour with rich aromas of spice, plump raisins and malt. On the palate there are hints of toffee and oak, with Sherry definition and a little smoke.

Strathisla Distillery. **63**

Glen Moray (La Martiniquaise)

Region: Speyside

Tel No: 01343 550900

Address: Bruceland Road, Elgin, IV30 1YE

Web Address: www.glenmoray.com

Originally a brewery, Glen Moray has now been producing whisky for over 100 years. The main road to Elgin, reportedly travelled by St Columba, King Duncan and Bonnie Prince Charlie, used to pass through the distillery, which is located in the shadow of Gallow Hill where executions used to take place. Glen Moray uses Bourbon casks to mature the whisky although some are finished in Madeira, Chardonnay and Chenin Blanc casks to create different expressions.

Colour, Nose and Tasting Notes:
Glen Moray 12 Year Old

Mid gold in colour, with aromas of vanilla and malt and some pear fruit. The taste is smooth, balanced and rounded with flavours of vanilla, malt and some toffee, leading to a long pleasing finish.

The Still House at Glen Moray Distillery.

Benromach (Gordon & MacPhail)

Region: Speyside

Tel No: 01309 675968

Address: Invererne Road, Forres, Moray, IV36 3EB

Web Address: www.benromach.com

Benromach is the smallest distillery in Speyside. Bought by Gordon and MacPhail in 1993 from the much larger United Distillers, it has had a chequered life with the distillery being mothballed twice, once in 1931 and again in 1983. There are only two members of staff employed at the distillery and they produce approximately 150,000-250,000 litres of spirit per year. Benromach was the first distillery to produce an Organic Whisky fully certified by the Soil Association. Gordon and MacPhail are continually trying new and innovative ways of adding different expressions to the brand and have released whiskies from single barley varieties and also Madeira and Port Pipes finishes.

Colour, Nose and Tasting Notes:
The Benromach 10 Year Old

Rich gold in colour, with light smoke on the nose, hints of Sherry and creamy vanilla, subtle spices such as ginger on the palate with ripe raisins and a delicate smokiness, all beautifully balanced and with a good length of finish.

Benromach Distillery. **67**

Dallas Dhu (Historic Scotland)

Region: Speyside
Tel No: 01309 676548

Address: Forres, Moray, IV36 2RR
Web Address: www.dallasdhu.com

The name means Black Water Valley and it was built in 1898 to produce whisky for the Glasgow firm of Wright and Greigs. They had a blend called Roderick Dhu of which Dallas Dhu formed the basis. After going into liquidation in 1921 it was sold to Benmore Distillers, who used it in their blends; it was also bottled under the name of Dallas Mhor. Dallas Dhu ceased production in 1983 mainly due to a lack of water and has since become a museum. Independent bottlings of Dallas Dhu can still be purchased although with each year that passes these will gradually deplete.

Colour, Nose and Tasting Notes:

Dallas Dhu 1982
(Gordon and MacPhail)

Pale yellow in colour, with fresh crisp cereal notes, gentle citrus notes on the palate mingled with honey sweetness. The finish is smooth and lengthy.

Dallas Dhu Historic Distillery, located just to the south of Forres. **69**

Glen Ord (Diageo)

Region: Northern Highlands

Tel No: 01463 872004

Address: Muir of Ord, Ross-shire, IV6 7UJ

Web Address: www.discovering-distilleries.com

Glen Ord is one of the last surviving distilleries north-west of Inverness, surrounded by fertile barley fields on the Black Isle, in the village of Muir of Ord. It has changed hands many times since it was established in 1838 by Thomas Mackenzie. Today it belongs to global company Diageo for whom it plays an important role as it has a substantial maltings that supplies malted barley to many of their distilleries. During its history it has produced whisky under several names, the most recent being Singleton of Glen Ord, bottled at 12 years.

Colour, Nose and Tasting Notes:
The Singleton of Glen Ord

Mid-gold in colour, this whisky has light floral notes, with Sherry and orchard apples on the nose. The palate is rich and smooth with dried prunes, Sherry and honey, a medium length finish with a hint of spice and nuttiness.

The exhibition area at Glen Ord Distillery shows how whisky used to be made. **71**

The Dalmore (Whyte and Mackay Ltd)

Region: Northern Highlands

Tel No: 01349 882362

Address: Alness, Ross-shire, IV17 0UT

Web Address: www.thedalmore.com

Nestling on the shores of the Cromarty Firth in Alness stands Dalmore Distillery. Owned for almost a century by the Clan Mackenzie, the stag motif on Dalmore bottles is taken from the Clan crest. The Mackenzies were friends with Charles Mackay and James Whyte of Glasgow and for many years Dalmore was sold to them for blending. In 1960 the family sold to Whyte and Mackay. Since then it has gone from strength to strength and in 2011 refurbished and re-launched the visitor centre, treating visitors to state-of-the-art tours.

Colour, Nose and Tasting Notes:
The Dalmore 12 year old

Rich gold in colour with a nose of old cut orange marmalade and rich steeped raisins. To taste, there is rich Sherry and spices with a long finish and just a whiff of vanilla.

This beautifully preserved 1950s-vintage Commer lorry makes a fine sight outside 73
The Dalmore Distillery, complete with valuable load!

Glenmorangie (Glenmorangie Co Ltd)

Region: Northern Highlands

Tel No: 01862 892477

Address: Tain, Ross-shire, IV19 1PZ

Web Address: www.glenmorangie.com

One of the oldest distilleries in production, there are records of distilling at Morangie farm as far back as the early 1700s, although it was in 1843 that a licence was acquired to produce whisky legally. Glenmorangie has famously tall stills, ensuring only the very lightest of vapours are distilled into spirit, making it one of the most popular single malts in Scotland. Glenmorangie also pioneered the use of a variety of wood finishes to create different expressions of the famous whisky. For example, the Quinta Ruban whisky is matured in American oak casks before being transferred to 'port pipes' from the Port and wine estates of Portugal.

Colour, Nose and Tasting Notes:

Glenmorangie Quinta Ruban 12 Year Old

Rich golden colour, there is the hint of rich dark chocolate, a whisper of orange and wood on the nose with a little spice. The palate is truly awakened with the richness of dark chocolate, mingled with walnuts and the sweetness of oranges with a long, lingering and silky finish.

Glenmorangie Distillery.

Clynelish (Diageo)

Region: Northern Highlands

Tel No: 01408 623000

Address: Brora, Sutherland, KW9 6LR

Web Address: www.malts.com

Clynelish was founded in 1819 by the Duke of Sutherland in the east-coast town of Brora. For many years it was only available privately, trade orders were refused! By 1933 the distillery had closed due to the Depression. It re-opened briefly between 1938 and 1941 when it closed again due to restrictions on the use of barley for making whisky during the Second World War. By the 1960s it had been refurbished and in 1967 a new distillery was built across the road and Clynelish moved. The original distillery was renamed Brora. This continued to produce whisky for a while but to a different recipe which was far more heavily peated. It has since closed and is now used for warehousing the Clynelish whisky.

Colour, Nose and Tasting Notes:
Clynelish 14 Year Old

Mid-gold in colour and a fragrant floral nose with hints of sea freshness, citrus elements and spices. The taste fills the mouth with smooth, rounded, slightly peaty flavours that lead on to hints of honey sweetness and Sherry.

Checking the stills at Clynelish Distillery.

Pulteney (Inver House Distillers)

Region: Northern Highlands

Tel No: 01955 602371

Address: Huddart Street, Wick, Caithness, KW1 5BA

Web Address: www.inverhouse.com

Old Pulteney Distillery is in the Caithness town of Wick. Known as the Maritime Malt, the distillery stands next to the harbour. Founded in 1826 by James Henderson, it is Scotland's most northerly mainland distillery. Built at a time when the town was not very accessible by road, the whisky was made using barley brought in by boat. Wick became famous for its silver and gold exports, silver from the herring boom (it was the busiest herring port in Europe at one point) and gold from its whisky! Steeped in history, this is a distillery that deserves a visit.

Colour, Nose and Tasting Notes:
Old Pulteney 17 Year Old

Rich gold in colour, the nose of this whisky is of autumn apples and pears, oak with subtle toffee. The taste is full bodied with vanilla, florals with ripe fruit, leading on to a long lingering finish.

78 Old Pulteney 12 Year Old.

Highland Park Distillery is the most northern of Scotland's distilleries, located on Orkney. It has an interesting history since being started by Magnus Eunson, a whisky smuggler in the late 1700s. In 1816 John Robertson, a former excise man who had arrested Magnus Eunson, took over production. Since then it has been in several different companies' ownership, culminating in being bought by the Edrington group in 1999. It produces several ages of single malt, the most popular being the 12 Year Old. It malts some of its own barley and the whisky destined to be used for single malt is always matured in Sherry casks, while the remainder used for blending is matured in Bourbon casks.

Colour, Nose and Tasting Notes:

Highland Park 12 Year Old

The colour of rich amber, with hints of honey, peat smoke and some orchard fruit on the nose. The palate is rich and smooth with gentle smoke, subtle Sherry with a warming long finish.

Published 2012 by Ness Publishing, 47 Academy Street, Elgin, Moray, IV30 1LR
Phone 01343 549663   www.nesspublishing.co.uk

Photographs © Colin Nutt except pp.4 & 55 © Chivas Brothers; pp.17, 31, 43, 47, 50, 53 & 77 © Diageo;
p.19 © Burn Stewart Distillers Ltd; pp.25, 29, 33, 35, 45 & 73 © Graham Ellis; p.27 © Tullibardine Distillery;
p.38 © Alex Gillespie; p.75 © Glemorangie Co. Ltd; p.79 © The Edrington Group; p.80 © Morrison Bowmore Distillers

Text © Penny Ellis
ISBN 978-1-906549-82-4

Front cover: pagodas at Dalwhinnie Distillery; p.1: at The Glenlivet Distillery; p.4: portrait of George Smith;
this page: Glen Garioch Distillery; back cover: Balvenie Distillery, Dufftown

For a list of whisky bars and shops please turn over >

Whisky Bars

EDINBURGH

Whiski Rooms, The Mound, 4–7 North Bank Street, Edinburgh, EH1 2LP

Whisky Shop (T) 0131 225 1532   Bar & Bistro (T) 0131 225 7224   www.whiskirooms.co.uk
Multi-award-winning whisky bar with a huge collection of Malt Whiskies and a really great atmosphere

GLASGOW

Lismore, 206 Dumbarton Road, Glasgow, G11 6UW (T) 0141 576 0103
This Bar has an impressive selection of Malt Whisky and features traditional music sessions. You will mix with locals and international travellers visiting to appreciate this venue. The stained glass windows tell the story of the Highland Clearances.

SPEYSIDE

The Highlander Inn, Craigellachie, Speyside, Banffshire, AB38 9SR (T) 01340 881446   www.whiskyinn.com
This Bar and Inn is in the centre of Speyside and has become internationally known by whisky lovers from all over the world. Expertly run with passion and dedication, it even has it own bottling unique to the Inn.

The Mash Tun, 8 Broomfield Square, Aberlour, Speyside, AB38 9QP (T) 01340 881771   www.mashtun-aberlour.com
The Mash Tun is located in the heart of Aberlour close to the old railway station and Speyside Way, so if you are walking this is an ideal resting point where you can taste a fabulous collection of Glenfarclas Malts.

Knockomie Hotel, Grantown Road, Forres, Moray, IV36 2SG (T) 01309 673146   www.knockomie.co.uk
Pleasant Inn, located on A940 just south of Forres with an extensive collection of Malts.